Written by **Andy Braun**

Illustrated by **Nils & Annie Guldberg**

For more information regarding permission, additional educational resources, and more, visit branchesband.com.
ISBN 978-1-7356228-4-2

Samson, he was big and strong
and God used him to right some wrongs

And wipe out many Philistines,
and he did that so many times!

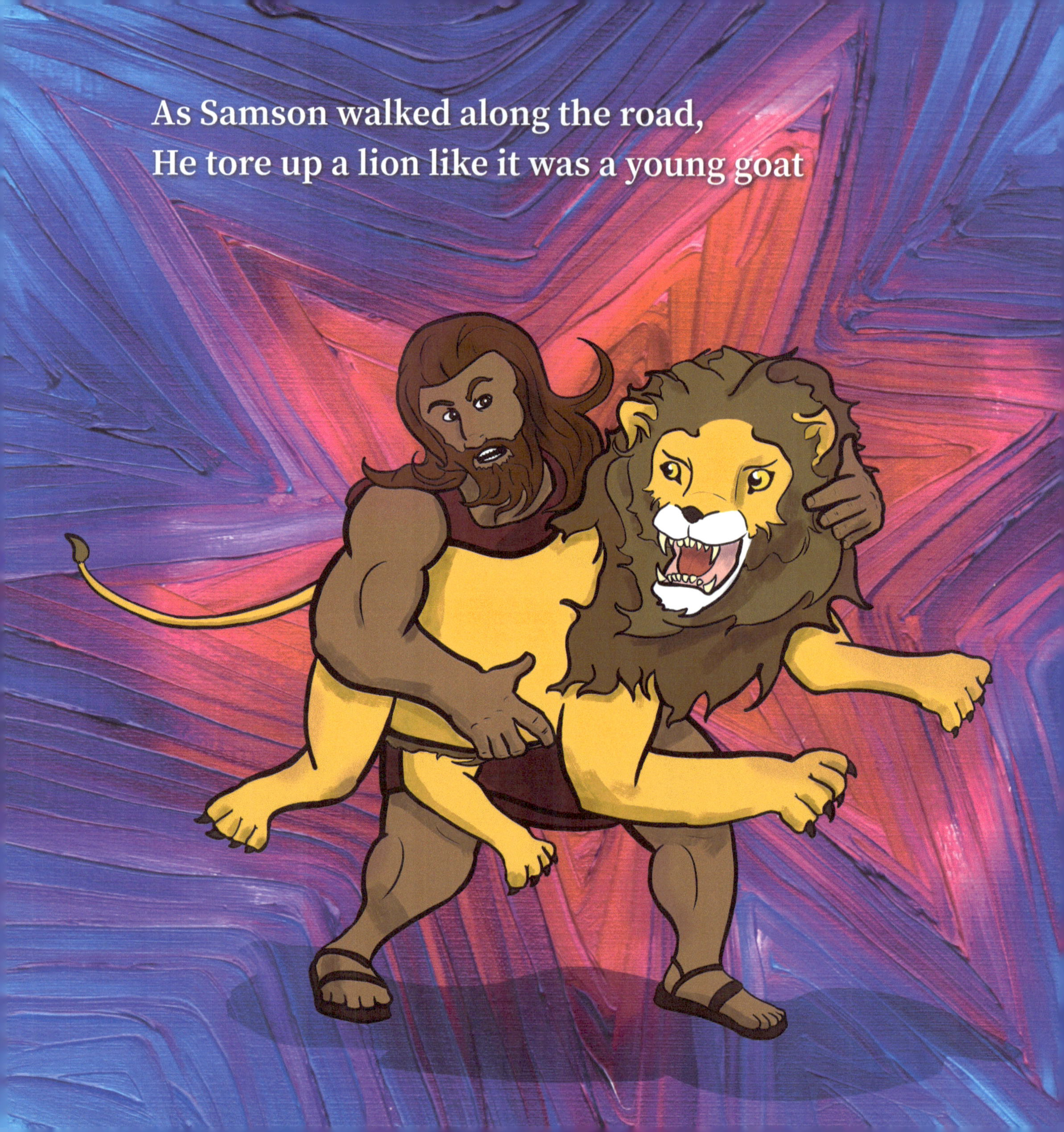

As Samson walked along the road,
He tore up a lion like it was a young goat

And the bees moved in to make a honeycomb,
So he scooped it out and gave his parents some.

Then he told this riddle to some Philistine guys
(And he made a bet with fancy clothes as the prize):

“Out of the eater, something to eat;
Out of the strong, something sweet.”

Well, the Philistines got to Samson's wife
And figured out the riddle,
causing Samson strife,

So he went and struck down thirty men
And brought back their clothes to settle up his debt.

Samson, he was big and strong
and God used him to right some wrongs

And wipe out many Philistines,
and he did that so many times!

Well, Samson's wife was given to another guy,
So he caught 300 foxes and he lit 'em on fire

And set ‘em loose to burn down all the crops in the land,
So the Philistines killed his wife and her old man.

Then Samson said, “I’ll get my revenge!”
And he attacked and slaughtered so many of them.

His friends from Judah asked him to behave,
So Samson played along;
they bound him up like a slave.

When they turned him over, he was good as dead,

But Samson tore his ropes and grabbed a donkey's head

And with that jawbone killed a thousand men
And said, "I've made donkeys out of all of them!"

Samson, he was big and strong
and God used him to right some wrongs

And wipe out many Philistines,
and he did that so many times!

Well, Samson fell in love with Delilah and then

The Philistines bribed her to betray her man.
They said, “Find out the secret of his strength and we
Will make you rich beyond your wildest dreams.”

Well, three times she tried

and three times he lied,

So Delilah cried
and Samson
finally complied

And they cut his hair
which had grown so long

And when Samson woke up, well, his strength was gone.

Well, they blinded Samson and they made him a slave,
But Samson cried out to the Lord and he prayed,

So the Lord gave him strength to do His will once more
And he brought down more Philistines than ever before!

Samson, he was big and strong
and God used him to right some wrongs
And wipe out many Philistines,
and he did that so many times!
SAMSON!

Andy Braun is a husband, father, and full-time traveling musician. He is passionate about reaching people with music and sharing God's Word in song. He received a BA in Communication from Wisconsin Lutheran College. It was there he met his wife, Rachel, and they have been blessed to do music full-time for the past 14 years (and counting!). Being a part of Branches Band has allowed Andy and Rachel to sing in all 50 states and Canada, as well as write many original Scripture-based songs and hymn arrangements. Andy is excited to collaborate with his good friends, Nils and Annie, and he thanks his wife, Rachel, for helping to bring this project to completion. Samson has been Andy's favorite Bible account since he was young and he is thrilled to present a children's book based on his original song about this unique historical figure! Learn more about Andy at andybraun.com.

Husband-and-wife team **Nils and Annie Guldberg** have been collaborating on creative projects for years. Nils Guldberg is a graphic designer, illustrator, and writer. Annie is a professional oil painter and art instructor. They worked on "Samson!" together from concept to completion: Annie painted the backgrounds in her signature swirling oil paints, and Nils illustrated the characters digitally. Nils and Annie met at Wisconsin Lutheran College (where Nils was roommates with Andy Braun!) and have been married for 15 years. In addition to their art adventures, Nils and Annie keep busy raising their two creative and energetic sons. You can see more of their work at NilsGuldberg.com and OilPainterAnnie.com.

Find the "Samson!" song and much more!

"Samson!" started out as a children's song on Branches Band's first children's album: "Let the Children Come to Me". You can find this album and songbook (as well as many other resources for your home, church, and classroom) at: branchesband.com

The text of this book is set in Source Serif Pro.
The illustrations are done in oil paints with digital character illustrations.

www.ingramcontent.com/pod-product-compliance
Lightning Source LLC
LaVergne TN
LVHW070205110826
845147LV00002B/508

* 9 7 8 1 7 3 5 6 2 2 8 4 2 *